Living Vedanta Series

Śraddhāvān Labhate Jñānam
Freedom from Distrust and Despair

तद्विद्धि प्रणिपातेन परिप्रश्नेन सेवया

Light of Vedanta Press. 2022

Swamini Svatmavidyananda

Arsha Vijnana Gurukulam
https://www.arshavg.org

ISBN: 978-1-5136-9736-9

Preface

I am very happy that Kate Herse and Kavita Meegama took the initiative to transcribe and edit a series of my talks on various topics. Their idea was to compile 9 or 10 talks into a one book. The coronavirus pandemic has brought a palpable immediacy to people's spiritual pursuits. Seen from this angle, perhaps it is more expedient to bring out these talks in the form of single booklets. This is the first of many in the series entitled "Living Vedanta." Several people helped with this project by generously contributing their time and skills. Kavita and Kate were very thorough in their edits. Additionally, I am thankful to Chris, Vivian, Sarah, Bhaskar and Lalita for their support and encouragement. Kathryn, Claudia and Joan gave wonderful suggestions, and helped with the final editing and proofreading.

I pray that seekers everywhere benefit from reading this book and be filled with the *śraddhā* needed for the study and assimilation of Vedanta.

Swamini Svatmavidyananda
Eugene, OR, USA
https://www.arshavg.org

Introduction

The Sanskrit word for doubt is *samśaya*. A mind given to chronic doubt and distrust is an impediment to gaining emotional maturity, which is essential for spiritual growth. At the beginning of the quest to understand the truth of oneself, there can be some doubt about how to proceed. This is natural. While one may be acutely aware of a niggling sense of discomfort with one's life choices, one may not know what one really wants. To compound matters, there is a plethora of choices presented in the spiritual marketplace, replete with leaders and saviors of all kinds, each touting their own brand of redemption. At this point, the doubting mind is a shield that protects one from getting carried away, from making a choice that is not conducive to one's quest.

Committing to a spiritual path is somewhat akin to buying a mirror. You go to the shop and stand in front of many mirrors, one after another. At this point, you are not really interested in looking at yourself; instead, you are examining the mirror carefully to see if it reflects your image authentically. If the mirror distorts your appearance even slightly, you reject it. After much deliberation, you decide on a mirror; you bring it home and hang it in your bedroom. The next morning, upon waking you go and stand in front of the new mirror. Now you are no longer testing the mirror –you are looking at yourself.

In the same manner, one explores various modalities and tries out different paths to ascertain the one which would provide the most suitable resolution for what one is seeking. After a period of exploration, when the *buddhi,* the intellect, has chosen a way forward, there is a sense of commitment, and the mind settles down. If this does not happen, it could mean that one is plagued by chronic doubt, which, in effect, holds one back from living life fully, and from progressing spiritually. When one constantly second-guesses oneself, the doubting mind stands in the way of self-knowledge, even destroying the quest itself.

The Bhagavad Gita says *samśayātmā vinaśyati* – the doubting one is destroyed. The root verb *naś* means to destroy. When you add the prefix *vi*, *vi* + *naś*, it means totally. The doubter perishes, meaning one is as good as destroyed. The doubting one is *upalakṣaṇa*, an indicator, for the place where the doubt resides, the mind, the *antaḥkaraṇa*. Therefore, 'the doubting one perishes' means that the place where the doubt resides, that kind of mind, perishes. 'Perishes' does not mean that one cannot recall anything – perhaps that would be a blessing in some ways– but when we say the mind 'perishes' it means the mind, the *antaḥkaraṇa,* is no longer available for the purpose for which it was made. What is the *antaḥkaraṇa* there for? Its sole purpose is to seek the truth of the self. The Vivekachudamani, a highly regarded Vedantic text, speaks of three things in this world that are extremely difficult to gain. They all start with 'M'. The first one is *manuṣyatva,* human birth. Next comes *mumukṣutva*, the desire to seek freedom from a sense of being trapped, by one's own body-mind complex all the way to the laws of the universe. The last 'M' is *mahapuruṣa-samśraya*, seeking refuge in a guru who can teach you that you are Brahman, the whole –not a part of the whole– but that you are the only source of existence and sentience in this universe. You are self-evident, and limitless –you are *saccidāndanda.*

Manuṣyatva

To be born as a human being is not an accidental event. On the contrary, human life is a manifestation of *puṇya*, merits, or good karma, earned in previous lives. Only when blessed by a human embodiment can one seek freedom from *saṃsāra*, which is best defined as a life of constant 'becoming.' From womb to tomb, human life is marked by the constant striving to 'become' someone, to gain something or another. The desire to 'become' more accomplished, more famous, more knowledgeable, or more acceptable consumes the entire life of a *jīva*, an individual. This constant striving to become limitless, due to self-ignorance, is the cause of fear, sorrow, and a sense of bondage, from which, once again, one struggles to be free.

Freedom from *saṁsāra* is contingent upon knowing the truth of oneself, for self-knowledge is what frees one from the 'freeze' of *saṁsāra*. *Saṁsāra* is indeed a total freeze. Everybody is, as it were, frozen like a statue as a result of being paralyzed by fear-based choices, thinking "If I do this, something bad will happen. If I do not do this, it might be still worse." One might conclude that by becoming a permanent statue one can escape karma. Not a chance! Karma continues to strike, whether you act or choose not to act. In fact, not acting, as Lord Krishna points out in the Bhagavad Gita, is also an action.

Human birth comes with the particular gift of the mind endowed with free will –the *antaḥkaraṇa* is analytical and is capable of making highly evolved choices and inferences. Adi Shankara points out that even animals can make inferences. If you ask the dog to sit, it will sit only if you have a treat in hand, because that is how it was trained. It will first look at your hand, and if the hand is empty, it will not sit. It is clever. The cow also makes inferences. If you approach her with some grass in hand, then she will eagerly walk towards you; on the contrary if she sees you carrying a stick, she will run away in fear.

The human capacity for inference and analysis, however, is much more evolved. Animals do not have the ability to enquire into the cause of fear or sorrow and seek a remedy. Moreover, they do not need Vedanta because they do not have problems of chronic sorrow or self-judgement. They do not have free will to judge themselves or others. By contrast, the human mind is simultaneously a blessing and a burden. It is totally self-aware and free, including being free enough to judge itself. The opening verse of the Amritabindu Upanishad says: *mana eva manuṣyāṇāṁ kāraṇaṁ bandhamokṣayoḥ*. The mind alone is the cause of both bondage and liberation for the human being. The same mind can either ensnare or liberate. Therefore, the first 'M', *manuṣyatva*, is human birth –the blessing of being born with a mind that is capable of knowing something is wrong in the large scheme of things, that one is in a vicious cycle of seeking the finite infinitely. Who said *saṁsāra* is not infinite? It certainly appears to be infinite, for as long as the problem of self-ignorance remains unresolved, *saṁsāra* continues forever! For the self-ignorant ones, *saṁsāra* is indeed the only infinity that they will ever know. Infinite striving to be free of bondage sandwiched between infinite births and infinite deaths is infinite *saṁsāra*. This is certainly not the kind of infinity we wish to pursue. In fact, we want to shake off this kind of infinity, because we have a different idea of it, where, effortlessly, we are content and whole.

Freedom, *mokṣa*, is intrinsic to our existence. Even the one who has never attended a Vedanta class knows that there is something that one deserves, something that appears out of reach. If you ask a lay person what they are seeking, they may say "happiness," they may say "peace." They may say that they want freedom from something or another, such as a chronic ailment or an oppressive person in their life. If one has a human mind, one knows that something is not right. Even the person unschooled in the ABCs of Vedanta –A for *ātman*, B for Brahman, C for *cit,* and so on– knows that something big is missing in life. All striving, therefore, arises for the purpose of compensating for this lack that is ultimately centered on oneself.

Mumukṣutva

Mumukṣutva, the desire for freedom, is the second of the three 'Ms'. A *mumukṣu* is a person endowed with a strong desire to be free of infinitely pursuing the finite. When you add the suffix *'tvam'* to the word *mumukṣu,* it transforms it into an abstract noun, *mumukṣu*–hood, or *mumukṣu*–ness. *Mumukṣutva* is difficult to gain. Instead of going about reproducing the pernicious cycle of *saṃsāra* life after life in the same way and meeting dead end upon dead end, the jaded-faded-*jīva,* stuck at the crossroads of many dead-ends, becomes, as it were, deadened to life itself. One is dead to the possibility of *mokṣa*, dead to the possibility of joyfulness. Even in the everyday life, one goes about one's tasks like a zombie, disconnected from oneself and others. Yet, due to some grace working overtime, one finds oneself shaking off this apathy and becoming acutely aware that something is wrong in the scheme of things, and whatever one does seems to exacerbate this problem of feeling bound to infinitely reproducing the finite. Numerous 'finites' do not the infinite make. Finite plus finite is just doubly finite. The person who knows this is a *mumukṣu*. The ability to see that there is something wrong in the way one is seeking is a great blessing. Not everyone is capable of arriving at this conclusion that the problem called *saṃsāra* is notional and is centered on the self. Lord Krishna points this out at the beginning of the seventh chapter of the Bhagavad Gita:

manuṣyāṇāṁ sahasreṣu kaścidyatati siddhaye ।
yatatām api siddhānāṁ kaścinmām vetti tattvataḥ ॥
Among thousands of people, one person seeks this freedom, and of the many seekers, one alone comes to know me as the truth of his or her self (7.3).

Mahāpuruṣa-saṁśraya

Taking refuge in a teacher is the third 'M'. *Mahāpuruṣa-saṁśrayaḥ* is knowing that one cannot seek the self on one's own, and that one needs help. This is in itself is a great blessing. A *mahāpuruṣa* is a guru, adept in self-knowledge, and, therefore, in a position to guide others. *Saṁśraya* is refuge. The *mahāpuruṣa* is not some kind of a savior who has dropped from the sky, or a self-made 'guru' of sorts. If you ask self-styled god-men or god-women, "How did you gain this knowledge," they commonly say, "I gained it *apne aap,*" meaning, they gained it all by themselves. About these *'apne-aap'* people, my guru, Pujya Swamiji, would jokingly say that he felt like telling them: "Please keep that knowledge all to yourself and enjoy it. Do not give it to us." Vedanta is an ancient body of knowledge of the self, handed down from teacher to disciple through sophisticated pedagogies that work to unseat self-ignorance and the misidentification of the self as the solely the body or mind. Studying with a teacher is the only way to gain this knowledge. Reading the Upanishads by oneself just does not work, because the infrastructure of self-ignorance, and its offspring in the form of doubt, distrust and despair impede the assimilation of its truth. It takes a period of committed exposure, of actively listening to the teachings before one can live this knowledge.

DIY Vedanta, do-it-yourself Vedanta, simply does not exist. Vedanta is effective only when it travels from the mouth of the teacher to the ears of the student. The disciples study with the teacher until they are steady in the knowledge. If they choose to take this forward and become teachers, then the next generation of students learn from them. This is known as the teaching lineage, *paraṁpara*. In this way, the lineage-based system of learning ensures that the focus is always on the transmission of the knowledge received from the teacher. That is why Vedanta is not a cult that is based on the personality of a given teacher. Instead it unfolds the nature of the cosmic person, the *puruṣa*, *Īśvara,* manifest as this vast *jagat,* through various names and forms.

Committed exposure helps overcome habitual patterns. The one who has had such exposure to Vedanta and has been able to gain mastery over the habitual patterns is the one who is qualified to teach. Such a teacher is the *mahāpuruṣa*. The guru is the one who– like the popular Indian dessert, the *gulab-jamun*– has soaked in the sweet vat of limitless oneness –the essence of the *śruti,* the teachings. The *gulab-jamun* is a popular dessert in India. It is fried ball of dough. If you try to taste this ball of dough, as soon as it comes out of the fryer, it is insipid. The ball has to be submerged overnight in sugar syrup, flavored with rose and cardamon essences. By the next morning, the *gulab-jamun* has soaked up the sugar syrup fully and is tasty to the core. Similarly, the aimless and anguished *jīva,* crying for help, is rescued from the hot oil of *saṁsāra*, by the compassionate guru. The *mahāpuruṣa* then drops the individual in the sweet syrup of the Upanishads, fragrant with the essence of oneness. The *jīva* has to stay deeply immersed in this knowledge. This is what we mean by committed exposure –immersing oneself in the knowledge until you can no longer make a distinction between knowledge and knower. This cannot happen without the *mahāpuruṣa*'s help. The word *saṁśraya* indicates a dedicated surrender to the teachings, and to the teacher, which suggests that being a drop-in *mumukṣu* is not enough to remove self-ignorance and the resultant notion that one is bound. The desire for freedom, *mumukṣā* has to be converted to *jijñāsā*, the yearning for knowledge.

The three 'M's', therefore, are very crucial to the seeker of self-knowledge. We do not have a control over *manuṣyatva,* birth as a human being, but we have some say over the other two, namely *mumukṣutva*, seeking freedom through discerning that one is far from comfortable reproducing the status-quo, and *mahāpuruṣa-saṁśraya*, seeking refuge in a teacher with the understanding that the freedom one wants is not gained by action, but by self-knowledge.

Two Scenarios

In many ways, the idea of dropping in and out of Vedanta according to one's whims seems ideal. Dropping in only seems expedient if one is not committed to grow in readiness –*tatparatā*. If one were to say that one does not want to grow spiritually, the *śāstra*, has a wonderful response. First it reveals the *prasāda*, the blessings, of cultivating trust and emotional maturity, and then it also demonstrates the lot of the people who do not make this choice. What choice exists, really speaking, when one craves wholeness and oneness with every fibre of one's being? It is a choice-less choice because the costs of not choosing to know yourself are too high. The *śāstra* offers two situations, where the choices are clearly presented. The Bhagavad Gita explains the first scenario thus:

śraddhāvān labhate jñānaṁ tatparaḥ saṁyatendriyaḥ I
jñānaṁ labdhvā parāṁ śāntim acireṇādhigacchati I I
The one endowed with devotion and commitment (to the guru and to the words of the śāstra), and mastery over the sense-organs gains knowledge of the self. Gaining this knowledge, one immediately gains absolute peace (4.39).

The second situation, by contrast, is dire:

ajñaścāśraddadhānaśca saṁśayātmā vinaśyati I
nāyaṁloko'sti na paraḥ na sukhaṁ saṁśayātmanaḥ I I
The one devoid of discrimination and trust (in the *śastra* and the guru), and the one endowed with a doubting mind perishes. For the distrustful one, this world is not there, nor the world beyond, nor happiness (4.40).

In the second verse, Lord Krishna appears to have an answer ready for the jaded individual, who might ask a hypothetical question "What happens if I do not have trust or commitment?"

Śraddhāvan Labhate Jñānam

This is a very oft-quoted, and important phrase in the Bhagavad Gita; it singles out *śraddhā,* as a crucial qualification for gaining self-knowledge. Among all the qualifications of an ideal student mentioned in the texts, *śraddhā* is of paramount importance. *Śraddhā* is the opposite of doubt. It is trust pending understanding –having an open mind that says, "I am willing to try this without prejudice." *Śraddhā* is reverential readiness to be led towards the understanding of oneself as the whole, as non-separate from the Lord, *Īśvara*. Faith in the teacher and the texts expounding the knowledge of the self, where one thinks, "if my teacher has understood this, then so can I," is *śraddhā*.

The cultivation of qualifications such as *viveka* (discrimination), *vairāgya* (letting go of impermanent ends), *śama* (a resolved mind), *dama* (disciplining the organs of action), *titikṣa* (forbearance), *uparati* (the ability to let go), *śraddhā* (the ability to trust), *samādhana* (focus), and finally *mumukṣutva* (the desire to be free) are critical for the seeker. *Śraddhā* has a special place in this list, because is like a master key. When you gain *śraddhā*, all the other qualifications are a shoo-in –they come of their own accord. This is the promise of the *śāstra*. All that is needed for the knowledge to take place is *śraddhā*. *Śraddhāvān*, the one who is endowed with *śraddhā* gains self-knowledge.

Any other kind of knowledge that you pursue can only take you so far –it can make you think you are an expert in an ever-growing and never-ending field, leaving you always in the unenviable place of playing catch-up. The pursuit of all other branches of knowledge, although essential, still falls within the range of *saṁsāra,* the infinite pursuit of the finite. Self-knowledge is the only quest that is finite in the sense that it leads to the discovery of oneself as infinite. *Śraddhā*, therefore, is crucial for discovering that the seeker and the sought are one.

The Debacle of Distrust

A person without *śraddhā* is known as *aśraddadhāna.* Such a person is also *ajña,* self-ignorant. In his commentary to this verse, Adi Shankara translates the the word *ajña* as *ānatmānam eva jānāti iti anātmajñaḥ; anātmajñāḥ eva ajñāḥ*. Those who do not know the *ātman*, the self, are indeed the ignorant ones. The direct translation of the word *ajña is 'na jānāti iti,'* the one who does not know. Adi Shankara takes this a step further and defines the one who is ignorant as the one who knows only the *anātman,* the non-self. The one who does not know the self is the one who knows everything but the self. Such a person is fixated on all kinds of time-bound objects in the universe to the detriment of oneself, the timeless subject.

Everyone is born ignorant of the self. When self-ignorance is accompanied by distrust, a*śraddhā*, it is a dangerous combination. An ignorant person, who is also distrustful, who does not have *śraddhā,* faith, in the knowledge, cannot be led. Such a person is *saṁśayātmā* –a chronic doubter. Doubt arises from ignorance and distrust. This deadly medley results in a sense of alienation. Over time, distrust, *aśraddhā,* leads to a DIY attitude, where one constantly tries to figure things out on one's own, including the knowledge of oneself, which is beyond the ken of the five senses and inference. Vedanta is an independent means of knowledge in the form of words revealed by the holy texts known as the Upanishads, and unfolded by teachers in the lineage. This is the only way to assimilate these teachings and understand the truth of the self.

What happens to a person without *śraddhā*? Being a quintessential doubter is tiring. Such a mind is destroyed. The mind, which can be the source of freedom, by knowing and reveling in its own glory, is instead bogged down by distrust and despair, and is incapable of seeking freedom from the notion of bondage. Hence, such a mind is as good as useless. If you want to destroy the mind, doubt alone is enough. In a way, it is more powerful than drugs or alcohol. It leaves one disenchanted, apathetic, and deadened to possibilities, because one will not allow oneself the privilege of assimilating the message of the ancient texts, which reveal the self as free of sorrow. One can be fortunate enough to have a human body, and a mind that knows something is wrong, and also be blessed with a guru. Yet, without cultivating trust, self-knowledge cannot not take place. Like a goal keeper, distrust repeatedly deflects all sources of help and keeps the *ahaṅkāra* mired in despair.

Overcoming Doubt with Trust

A mantra in the Sama-Veda says, *śraddhayā aśraddhāṃstara* –cross distrust by building a bridge of *śraddhā,* trust. How can one cross over distrust using trust? Already there is doubt, which is absence of trust. So how can one cross the sea of doubt with the bridge of trust? If one is a doubter, how can one manufacture *śraddhā* to cross over the doubt?

This is possible because *śraddhā* is already one's nature. To understand what trust is, one does not have to go very far, except to look back at one's own childhood. Anybody who has held a small child can sense its trust, its *śraddhā.* The child, who is completely helpless and dependent, is endowed with total trust for its primary caregivers. Even if they behave like primary 'scare-givers,' the infant will continue to trust them. As the child grows, it notices various inconsistencies in the caregivers. For example, the mother either 'smothers' or 'others' the child, while the father moves farther away from its affections. Such inevitable experiences make the *śraddhā* slowly recede from the heart. The child develops an armor of distrust as a survival mechanism to face the caregivers and the world it confronts. This *śraddhā* has to be as-though cultivated again – cultivated 'as-though' because it is there, but is layered with the dust of distrust. The *śraddhā* has to be recalled and rescued from the debris of doubt and despair. One reconnects with the trust that has become as-though obfuscated from experiences of repeated disappointment of failed trust in fallible and finite beings. Constantly fixing on the finite for gaining the infinite also negatively impacts *śraddhā*.

Loss of Trust

Once, as the story goes, a man ate a lot of spicy things that he knew would not agree with him and would wreak havoc on his digestive system. He binged on fried snacks like samosas and pakoras along with a spicy sauce made of hot chillies. He followed this act by eating an entire tub of ice cream. Unsurprisingly, he had burning sensations in the chest and stomach, leaving him writhing in discomfort. He kept saying, "Come on, where are you, O ice cream! Please come and cool off this tummy. Why are only the hot and spicy things talking in there right now?" The cultivation of *śraddhā* is somewhat like this. Like the ice cream that was overtaken by the spicy snacks, *śraddhā* is as-though lost because of the process of growing up in a complicated world. This process of losing trust is a natural part of the emotional growth cycle of the human being. In other words, to be disappointed is natural. If you have never been disappointed, you are not a human being. Disappointed and dejected is how one grows up. One cannot be all starry-eyed, bushy-tailed, jumping around like a permanent Easter bunny. It is just not realistic.

In fact, life is full of disappointments. You strive hard for a promotion, but your co-worker is the one who gets it. Your colleague then says happily, "I do not know why I got this promotion; honestly, I don't think I really deserve it," thereby sprinkling salt in the gaping wound of your dejection. It is almost as though there is an overarching law: of all that you do not want, you will definitely get multiple helpings; and whatever you do want badly, is not only elusive, but routinely goes to someone else who you think does not deserve it at all. This is the law. Murphy's Law reigns.

If anything can go wrong in one's life, it certainly will. In the beginning everyone has *śraddhā*. In babyhood, everyone is very trusting. After the trust is repeatedly broken, the child starts to withdraw. This is a protective mechanism. Another survival mechanism is flight –to be in denial and to go to one's 'happy place' in one' imagination. Sometimes the coping mechanism is a moping mechanism, as in the constant feeling of victimization. These are some instances of how one loses *śraddhā* in life. In effect, by the time one reaches adulthood, one does not trust anyone easily.

Śraddhā has to be re-cultivated because it was very much there before the hurtful life experiences of the past. In adulthood, *śraddhā* is there as a latent possibility. Just like the story of the man who said, "Come on ice cream, where are you? Cool off this acidity." In the same manner, the acidic, acerbic experiences of growing up and being constantly disappointed by life, by karma, have to be resolved and integrated by regaining the ability to trust, again. Though one is born with complete trust, losing that trust is not all that difficult. All it takes is for the young parent to accidentally drop the baby.

In Florida there is a highly skilled ayurvedic doctor who is an expert at reading people's pulses, and knowing things about their early childhood. He can sense a lot of things, just by touching a person's wrist. Over time, he has surprised many people with his insights. One time he felt the pulses of a man and asked him: "Did your mother accidentally drop you in childhood?" The patient did not know the answer, but later checked with his mother, and the mother said, "Yes, I never told you this, but I dropped you down a flight of stairs when you were nine months old."

Being dropped as a baby is enough for the *śraddhā* to drop. Even though the child may be outwardly smiling, there is a stone wall surrounding the heart. Then, when the child goes to school, more *śraddhā* gets dropped because the friends it trusts will abandon it and the teachers that it trusts may have no time for it. Like this, the *śraddhā* is constantly dropped. Even before school, there are siblings. Each time they pull your hair or snatch your toys *śraddhā* drops.

You then go to middle school –*śraddhā* drops. You go to high school, and *śraddhā* definitely drops some more. Then you go to college, and *śraddhā* drops even further. Whatever *śraddhā* remains definitely drops after you get married. The scales fall from the eyes. "What did I think you were? What did you turn out to be?" each spouse wonders about the other. *Śraddhā* just drops, drops, drops. When the children become teenagers, the *śraddhā* drops even further as the parents wonder, "How can you behave like this? How could we have given birth to something like this?" If you have a job, *śraddhā* drops. If you do not have a job, *śraddhā* drops a bit more. If you have an active social life, *śraddhā* drops. If you do not have a social life, *śraddhā* drops. The dropping of *śraddhā* is a universal life-experience, and the story of one's survival.

This lost trust has to now be rebuilt. We rebuild *śraddhā* by focusing on that which is worthy of trust. At first it appears as though all the things that one banked on have given way. Starting with the dysfunctional caregivers right up to the present, all things and people that one leaned on in babyhood, in childhood, in youth, in adulthood or in old-age were unworthy because in itself each entity was finite and fallible. Despite their best efforts, the parents were tired and distracted; the siblings were self-centered, and the teachers partial to someone else. In adulthood, the boss was a control freak, and the significant other did not turn out to be all that significant. The children that one banked on for companionship and care in old age grew to be distant and disappointing. In short everything and everyone that one trusted turned out to be infallibly fallible.

The Quest for the Infallible

If one attempts to rekindle lost trust by continuing to fixate on all things fallible, one is bound to have the same outcome of increased frustration and despair. A jaded *jīva*, a disappointed person, is not a *śraddhāvān*. Such a person is best described as deluded and lacking in discrimination. The rebuilding of *śraddhā* has to happen while keeping in view the innate human quest for the infallible. Is there something that is infallible? If so, what is it? The Upanishads reveal that the infallible cannot be located outside you. The infallible is the limitless Brahman, the cause of the universe, inseparable from you, and the truth of your nature.

This sounds incredibe. One can think: "Oh, but how can I be infallible?" We are not talking about you, the *ahaṅkāra*, the I-notion identifying with a specific body-mind-sense complex. On the contrary, the *śāstra* refers to the truth of the self as Brahman, the sentient existence that limitlessly pervades not only the body-mind-sense complex, but the entire universe of names and forms.

Brahman is transcendental and immanent. From the transcendental standpoint, there is no fallibility or finitude, because Brahman, the singular, non-dual sentient presence that pervades everything, lends its very being to all things in this universe, without 'becoming' any one thing. From the immanent standpoint Brahman is invoked as invariably present in the form of the *jagat*, the universe, as the Lord, as *Īśvara*. In our tradition, we do not view the Lord as an entity separate from creation. In fact, the creation is non-separate from the creator, who is tangibly manifest in all aspects of creation, including the various laws that govern the universe. In other words, the laws of the universe are not commandments of *Īśvara*, but the very manifestations of *Īśvara*. Put differently, the question is not "Did *Īśvara* create the hurricane?" Rather, we learn to see that this is what *Īśvara* is. In fact, all that is, is *Īśvara*. The hurricane, like every other natural phenomenon, is a manifestation of *Īśvara*. This is why I think the word "hurricane" should be spelled as "Hari-came!"

Viewed from the standpoint of the body-mind-complex, one is indeed finite, fallible, and helplessly subject to the laws of the universe, including the laws of karma. There is a yawning chasm between the-world-as-it-is, the objective world of names, forms, and phenomena; and the-world-as-I-really-want-it-to-be, the subjective world of individual preferences, prejudices and projections. The trust lost due to disappointment is rediscovered by making the conscious choice to be in harmony with the laws, and to see the universe as it is, rather than how one wishes it to be. This means settling accounts with *Īśvara* by growing into a place of acceptance of the infallible.

How can we say that *Īśvara* is infallible? We cannot. In fact, such a contention would be a set-up for nursing more resentment and distrust. "*Īśvara* is infallible" would be a purely subjective expression, depending upon how many personal favors one feels the Lord has granted in one's life. If, for instance, my life is unfolding exactly how I want it to be, then I have no problem saying that *Īśvara* is infallible. However, when my desires are unmet then, very quickly, *Īśvara* becomes fallible.

Turning the sentence on its head is a better understanding of the nature of *Īśvara* as revealed by the *śāstra*. Therefore, we say: that which is infallible is *Īśvara*. To put it differently, starting from one's own background, whenever one confronts anything that is inevitable, or beyond one's control, one is face to face with *Īśvara*. That which is inevitable is then seen as an expression of a vast order, which includes one's anger, frustration, distrust, and disappointment. Understanding this truth and rediscovering *śraddhā* requires emotional maturity.

Vedanta is wonderful because it brings everything back to you. There is no magic wand with which the teacher can touch you on the head after which you suddenly have self-knowledge. Nothing can replace the inner work that one has to do. You regain *śraddhā* by learning to trust *Bhagavān*, to trust the infinite source manifest in the form of infallible orders in the universe, which includes your own distrust. This *Bhagavān* cannot disappoint you. By shifting the locus of one's trust from all that is finite and fallible to the infinite and the infallible, one regains *śraddhā*.

The Infallible is *Īśvara*

As a first step, one trains oneself to be an objective witness to all mistrust and fears. Viewed from the vantage point of the psychological order, it is easy to see that this distrust is universal. One is not alone. Knowing this itself is a big relief. Next, one can see that the loss of trust is not a random event. There are reasons for distrust –it makes sense. There is a logic here, which is included in the vast order called psychology. When we can talk of vast patterns, we are having "darshan" of *Bhagavān* –we are one with *Īśvara* existing as the order that studies the human mind, including the causes of grievances and distrust.

One takes the bundle of grievances to the altar that is infallible. Perhaps this is why it is called 'altar' –because it has the power to 'alter' our distrust. The altar is a receptacle for one's pains and sorrows. Placing all disappointments at this altar causes them to become spiritualized and get embraced by the limitless.

Spiritualize, *Īśvar*-ize, your grievances. When you do this, you will see that there is a law behind all this, that it has very little to do with you. It is the law of karma that is at work. Therefore, that one was dropped down a flight of stairs as a baby is, ultimately, not the fault of the parents. It is karma.

Īśvara as the law of karma is very creative. Once, as a young adult, I was at a *navarātrī* celebration. Half the attendees wished to sing bhajans before dinner was served, and the other half wished to eat first and then sing bhajans. I thought that it would be better to have bhajans before *bhojan*, but I did not wish to disappoint the people who wished to eat first so they could leave early. I said a silent prayer: "O *Bhagavan*, I wish you would just tap me on the head and assure me that this is the right thing to do." Suddenly, somebody needed help to put a dish she had brought into the fridge. Since her hands were full, I got up to open the door of the fridge. People had brought many things for the dinner. One of them was a 5-gallon plastic container of apple juice that was perched out of sight atop the fridge. As I opened the door of the fridge, the enormous apple juice container got dislodged, fell on my head, and rolled on to the floor. It took a couple of seconds to recover from the shock, but after that I could not help but laugh. *Bhagavān* is infinitely creative. I said, "Tap me on the head," and I got an *Īśvara*-sized 5-gallon container tap.

The second step involves directing the trust towards the infallible. You trust that which is infallible, because it cannot disappoint, and because it is in the form of universal laws. A karmic law simply is what it is –it is not out to get you, and that is why you cannot take it personally. You discover trust by making the infallible the recipient of your trust. One learns to allow all grievances to rest at the altar of the infallible. This is because there is no place else to take them where they will be received without censure, resentment, or retaliation. If you try airing out all your grudges with 'significant others,' in your life, the word 'significant' will soon drop from the compound, and significantly 'other' your loved ones from you. The longer the grievances and hurts are left unprocessed, the more they fester and vitiate the present moment. Therefore, it is best to take grievances back to the source from whence they came.

The altar that is *Īśvara,* invoked in any name, form, or gender, is the burial ground for moldy grievances, the cemetery for leftover grudges and hurts past their prime. You are allowed to have tombstones for each one of them; there is no problem with that. You can even visit them sometimes, but it is good to remember that they are no longer alive, and they do not have the power to haunt you, even on Halloween. Such is the power of the altar of surrender. How is one able to bury these grievances once and for all?

One sees the larger picture here in the form of one's own karma and makes peace with karma as it is. It is, after all, a law, which is infallible. It is a manifestation of *Bhagavān*. When grudges and grievances, starting with hurts from early childhood to the present day, are ceremonially buried, then space arises for *śraddhā* to spontaneously emerge and for one to become a *śraddhāvān*. This is what it means to regain lost trust. In order to regain a trusting temperament, which is one's own nature, one makes a repast of the past.

Reclaiming Trust

This peacemaking exercise with past grievances allows one to prepare the heart for the pursuit of self-knowledge. Acceptance of what cannot be altered helps one to commit to the teachings of the Upanishads that reveal one's nature as unaffected by fear and sorrow. One can finally be free from a life of constantly identifying with the finite. Becoming *śraddhāvān,* although an important step, is not enough. Being a *śraddhāvān* is like wearing a tuxedo. When someone dons a tuxedo, it is assumed that the person is going out for a formal engagement. Just as it is strange to wear a tuxedo just to sit at home, so too, being *śraddhāvān* without seeking self-knowledge is a futile effort. Therefore, one seeks a teacher belonging to a sound *paraṁpara*, a lineage that does not distort the words of the Upanishads. Only then will the study of the *śāstra* bless the student to awaken from the stupor of self-ignorance, leading to the discovery of oneself as already free from *saṃsāra*.

At the beginning of the quest, a *sādhaka*, seeker, starts to relate to the teacher with trust. When the guru does not abuse the trust, the relieved student hangs on to the teacher as though life depended on it. Over time, retaining the love and care for the teacher, one graduates in one's spiritual journey to direct the trust one has cultivated for the guru, towards the *pramāṇa,* the sacred texts, which are the means of knowing the truth of oneself. This can only happen when one is able to resolve, or at least have the ability to put aside, the painful experiences of the past. Otherwise unresolved past experiences vitiate the teaching atmosphere and interfere in the assimilation of the knowledge. All too often the guru becomes a sitting duck, a target, for unresolved hurts and authority issues that are continuously projected onto the teacher by the student. That is why in the tradition, we have the prayer, *tvameva mātā ca pitā tvameva*. We revere the guru and say, "You alone are the mother, you alone are the father." In this way, one learns to let go of the pains connected to one's parentage. One grows by learning to see them as part of one's karmic trajectory, in which there are no accidents, only incidents that are, at times, difficult to comprehend.

Śraddhā is allowing the *ahaṅkāra*, the I-ness to settle down. This is as much part of the learning as the study of the Upanishads and other texts of the tradition. The onus is on you. You have to allow yourself to be re-parented in the light of the teachings, for which you have to be available to be taught. The cultivation of *śraddhā* is not linear; rather, it is like playing a game of snakes-and-ladders. No matter how high you go, there are pitfalls along the way. When you reach the number 99 you are greeted by the open maw of a colossal python that leads you all the way down to square number one. That is where, I suppose, the expression, 'back to square one' came from. Despite encountering setbacks in the cultivation of *śraddhā*, you have to persevere and overcome the pitfalls of stubborn projections and transferences. In this way, one grows into becoming a committed student of Vedanta. It is a journey, alright, but it need not be a painful one. If one is ready it is an enjoyable journey. How can one be ready? Really speaking, it is recognizing the fact that one is sick of being a mistrustful person –it is as simple as that. If one is completely revulsed by something, it becomes easy to overcome it. This is what readiness to discover *śraddhā* entails.

Refining *Śraddhā*

As *śraddhā* gets more refined and evolved, it is turned towards the infallible in the form of the *pramāṇa*, the means of knowledge, wielded by the guru. The word '*pramāṇa*' means words of the *śāstra*, handled by the teacher. That is where the *śraddhā* is directed. The trust, *śraddhā,* is not directed towards the personality of the guru, as such, because that is, again, a setup for disappointment. This is a really important lesson to learn. Transcending the personality of the guru one sees the *puruṣa, Īśvara,* in the guru. It is the same *puruṣa,* which the Upanishads reveal as the truth of yourself. Ultimately, there is no difference between you and the guru –the *mahāpuruṣa* that you seek is you. The *puruṣa –sarvān pūrayati iti–* the one who inhabits everything, the one who completes everything, is you. Since, as yet, one is unable to see this in oneself, one invokes *Īśvara* in the teacher. This is the difference between a cult and a well-established lineage of non-duality known as *advaita-paraṁpara*. In the imparting of the teaching, the emphasis is on the lineage, not on a single personality. No matter how charismatic any teacher might be, the focus on the lineage ensures that the teaching gets faithfully handed over to the disciple, who then can see herself/himself as non-separate from the whole. As the knowledge is assimilated, one sees the guru in oneself. You transcend the personality and see that you are one with the person revealing the knowledge of the self. If one focuses primarily on the personality of the guru, then the guru becomes the most fallible being on earth. The guru has quirks; the guru falls sick, the guru ages and becomes feeble. All it takes for the *śraddhā* to jump out of the window is for the guru to be seen picking at the teeth, or belching after lunch. "What can such an uncouth person teach me," one might just wonder and back off quietly.

The story of the teacher, Raikva, in the Brihadaranyaka Upanishad, illustrates this point nicely. Janashruti, a wealthy king, was dissatisfied with himself. He was a *mumukṣu*. He finally sensed the need to study with a teacher, and commanded his army, "Go scour the mountains, go scan the forests. Catch hold of the best guru and bring him to me. I want to study the *śāstra*." The king's men set forth to accomplish this task. In the course of their quest, they encountered several teachers, all of whom refused to teach the king. They all said that they were not the best; the one known as Raikva was the best teacher. "We do not know what Raikva knows," they all said, adding that since Raikva would never go to the palace, the king would have to approach him.

The king, along with a large retinue duly set forth to seek Raikva. After some effort, they found an unkempt and disheveled man living under a broken-down chariot. Raikva did not fit the mold of a guru by any stretch of the imagination. His clothes were in tatters, and his body was full of sores and scabs that he was constantly scratching as he conversed with the king. We have to applaud Janashruti's *śraddhā* because he was able to see past all this, and ask for self-knowledge.

Through this story we learn that in focussing solely on the physical form or the personality of the teacher one can miss the teaching entirely. The physical attributes of the teacher are there for the sake of *vyavahāra,* for the purpose of being able to relate to the teacher. One can only relate through names and forms. The challenge, here, is to understand oneself as ultimately formless, even as one relates to the form of the teacher. This is where *śraddhā* plays a salient role, because *śraddhā* helps you overlook things that do not really matter, and process the triggers that might come in the way of interacting with the teacher.

Commitment and Self-Discipline

The verse from the Bhagavad Gita that we have been discussing mentions two other qualities that complement *śraddhā, namely, tatparatā,* commitment, and *saṃyatendriyatva,* discipline with regard to the sense organs. A *tatpara* is a person of committed pursuit, for whom there is no goal other than self-knowledge.[1] The word *tat* means 'that', and it generally refers to Brahman. Brahman is 'that' because, being the truth of the self, it cannot be objectified. It is intangible and therefore appears to be far away from oneself. A *tatpara* is one for whom Brahman is the only goal.

---

[1] *Tad eva paraḥ yasya saḥ, tatparaḥ.*

This shows that *śraddhā* must be accompanied by a committed pursuit of self-knowledge.

What happens when one has *śraddhā*, but is not particularly committed to the teaching? Such a person might simply adore the guru and wish to hang out with the teacher all the time, without really being interested in what the guru has to offer. In this scenario, even if the student does not get bored, the guru certainly will! It is not very different from the popular concept of heaven, where the person goes after death, and sits in front of God. After a while, even God will tell the ardent devotee, "Enough! get up please, and for heaven's sake go do something else." One cannot be guru-gazing all the time. After all, one has a human mind. It naturally wanders; it judges and critiques everything, including the teacher. *Śraddhā* without commitment easily gets dissipated.

This is why the verse from the Gita emphasizes the need for one to evolve from guru-gazing to grazing in the garden of the Gita, and ingesting the verses of oneness, which the guru has revealed. That is how one practices commitment. The commitment is not to the physical persona of the guru, for the form is just a medium for the transmission of knowledge. The commitment is to the *pramāṇa,* the pedagogy of unfoldment of the teaching, that the guru gracefully carries and operates.

The last attribute mentioned in this verse is *saṁyatendriyatva,* mastery over organs of action and sense organs. If readiness is there, but the sense organs are busily consuming the finite, it is not of much use; If there is commitment but no *śraddhā*, the person might become a dedicated researcher of Vedanta, with little interest in allowing it to be self-transformative. Such people are perhaps intrigued by the number of times the word '*puruṣa*' appears in the Vedas. This is purely a counting exercise. The point is to understand the meaning of the word '*puruṣa*'. These are people who become the statisticians of the Upanishads, and pontificate on questions such as "How many times does the word 'Janaka' occur in all the sacred texts? Are all of them the same Janaka?" A mind given to such flippancy is a mind whose potential is totally wasted.

A committed exposure to the knowledge alone gives fulfillment. We are talking of uncovering the nature of oneself. If one's nature is already trusting, free and happy, one has to discover it, for which one needs self-knowledge. That is how the *ātma-ajñāna,* self-ignorance, is banished. It requires *śraddhā,* for which one has to be ready for a committed pursuit, where one does not just keep dropping in and out, and does not let anything get in the way. For the purpose of this committed pursuit, all the other pursuits of the sense organs are reined in by consuming mindfully. In this way, one becomes a *saṁyatendriya*.

If one is unable to have *śraddhā*, the teaching is not assimilated. Forget about the teachings –they are not even on the person's radar– but even regular life becomes miserable for such people. Tortured by distrust, they end up hurting the ones they love. They are, for instance, unable to trust their own spouses, children, or co-workers; they are constantly suspicious, and incapable of giving anyone the benefit of doubt. Such people are also subject to control issues due to their own insecurities.

One has to learn to manage one's doubts in the household, and at work, before one can eliminate doubts at the level of teacher and teachings. Therefore, the household and the workplace are training grounds for developing trust. Only after that, one can go on to cultivate *śraddhā* in the guru and in the knowledge of the self. The distrustful person without *śraddhā* cannot enjoy even a moment of peace. For such a person who is restless and has a doubting mind, where is the happiness? The doubting person is utterly miserable; such people cannot even have the privilege of enjoying their lives and their loved ones, what to talk of gaining absolute joy and peace that is centered on the self. It is simply a pipe dream.

Relative and Absolute Śānti

There is no doubt that when *śraddhā* is accompanied by the committed pursuit of knowledge and mastery over the sense organs, self-knowledge is definitely gained. What happens when one gains the knowledge? The Bhagavad Gita says that the person also gains absolute peace.

There are two kinds of peace discussed in the *śāstra*. The first kind is peace that exists between two upsetting events. The manifestation of this *śānti* is contingent upon the occasional absence of distress and strife in one's life. This kind of *śānti* comes and goes. It is dependent on numerous external factors, such as the weather, the behavior of people in one's life, and internal factors, such as the state of one's own mind. If there is disturbance in any of these realms, it greatly upsets one's peace of mind. Through disciplining the mind and the sense organs, one can train oneself to enjoy relative *śānti*. In fact, this is a prerequisite for gaining absolute *śānti,* which is *jñānaprasāda,* the blessing of self-knowledge.

The second kind of peace, *parā śānti,* absolute peace, is not a state of mind. Rather, it is the discovery of the nature of the self as without a second and, therefore, totally free from agitation. Absolute peace is gained through the understanding of the self as Brahman, the source of everything. One is free by knowing oneself as whole and limitless. Despite being confronted by disturbances from within or without, one is unaffected by them. Absolute peace is not dependent upon maintaining a particular mental condition, or controlling one's surroundings. It is unopposed to both cacophony and silence, for it transcends all dichotomies. Being the very nature of the self, absolute peace is not temporary tranquility generated by music or meditation, but the very nature of oneself as limitless awareness. A person enjoying relative peace can gain absolute *śānti* through the committed pursuit of self-knowledge.

Conclusion

The journey from distrust to the knowledge of oneself as whole and free, hinges on the deliberate ousting of doubt and the re-cultivation of trust that was lost in childhood. The steps are clear. At first, one recognizes the ways in which chronic doubt can paralyze and impede one's progress. Therefore, one cultivates *śraddhā*, faith pending understanding, and seeks a teacher to expound the vision of the Upanishads. Next, one directs the *śraddhā* towards the teacher and the texts and makes oneself available for the teaching to take effect. Finally, one refines *śraddhā* by disciplining the mind and sense organs. These steps lead to relative peace, *śānti* which, in turn, strengthens one's preparedness and resolve to pursue the knowledge Vedanta, and assimilate its vision of oneself as limitless, free, naturally tranquil and incapable of being disturbed.

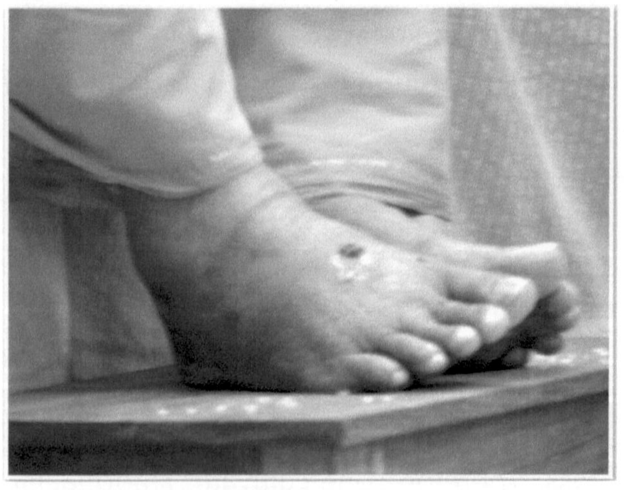

–OM TAT SAT–

ABOUT THE AUTHOR

Swamini Svatmavidyananda is a long-term disciple of Pujya Sri Swami Dayananda Saraswati. She is the acharya of Arsha Vijnana Gurukulam based in USA and India. She also teaches regularly at the Arsha Vidya Gurukulam in Saylorsburg, PA. For more information and to participate in online and in-person retreats, please visit the following sites:

Website: https://www.arshavg.org;
Youtube: https://www.youtube.com/Svatmavidyananda;
Podcasts: https://www.arshagurukulam.podbean.com

www.ingramcontent.com/pod-product-compliance
Ingram Content Group UK Ltd.
Pitfield, Milton Keynes, MK11 3LW, UK
UKHW041844190726
13854UKWH00002B/705